Pebble
Plus

The Skinny on
Hot Dogs

by Catherine Ipcizade

Consulting Editor: Gail Saunders-Smith, PhD

Consultant: Professor Art Hill
Department of Food Science
University of Guelph

CAPSTONE PRESS
a capstone imprint

Pebble Plus is published by Capstone Press,
151 Good Counsel Drive, P.O. Box 669, Mankato, Minnesota 56002.
www.capstonepub.com

Books published by Capstone Press are manufactured with paper
containing at least 10 percent post-consumer waste.

Library of Congress Cataloging-in-Publication Data
Ipcizade, Catherine.
   The skinny on hot dogs / by Catherine Ipcizade.
      p. cm.—(Pebble plus. Favorite food facts)
   Includes bibliographical references and index.
   Summary: "Full-color photographs and simple text present fun facts about hot dogs"—Provided by publisher.
   ISBN 978-1-4296-6661-9 (library binding)
   1. Frankfurters—Juvenile literature. 2. Cooking (Frankfurters)—Juvenile literature. I. Title. II. Series.
TX749.I63 2012
641.6'6—dc22   2011000373

Editorial Credits
Katy Kudela, editor; Heidi Thompson, designer; Svetlana Zhurkin, media researcher; Sarah Schuette, photo stylist;
   Marcy Morin, scheduler; Laura Manthe, production specialist

Photo Credits
Alamy/Blend Images, 15
Capstone Studio/Karon Dubke, cover, 1, 10–11, 13, 19, 20–21, 21 (top right)
Corbis, 6–7; Bettmann, 9
Shutterstock/Karin Hildebrand Lau, 4–5
Svetlana Zhurkin, 16–17

Note to Parents and Teachers

The Favorite Food Facts series supports national social studies standards related to people,
places, and culture. This book describes and illustrates hot dogs. The images support early
readers in understanding the text. The repetition of words and phrases helps early readers learn
new words. This book also introduces early readers to subject-specific vocabulary words, which
are defined in the Glossary section. Early readers may need assistance to read some words
and to use the Table of Contents, Glossary, Read More, Internet Sites, and Index sections of
the book.

Printed in the United States of America in North Mankato, Minnesota.
032011   006110CGF11

Table of Contents

Fun on a Bun

Fire up the grill! Enough hot dogs are sold each year to feed each American 60 of them! Summer is the favorite season for roasting hot dogs.

Inventing Hot Dogs

People in Frankfurt, Germany, say they made the first hot dog in 1487. They named it the "frankfurter." Later the name changed to "hot dog" or "frank."

7

In 1871 Coney Island got its first hot dog stand. More than 3,000 hot dogs on buns sold the first year! Today New York City has hundreds of hot dog stands.

By the 1940s, hot dog stands lined the streets of New York City. ⟶

9

How It's Made

Beef, pork, and spices make up most hot dogs. Some hot dogs have chicken or turkey. Meatless hot dogs are made of soy.

Corn dogs became a Texas fair food in 1942. These hot dogs are dipped in cornmeal batter and fried. Sticks make them an easy food to carry.

Imagine That!

Hot dogs are an easy food

to grab on the go.

The Chicago O'Hare Airport

sells 2 million hot dogs a year!

How do you eat a hot dog
and french fries in one bite?
In Korea people eat
french fry-covered hot dogs.

Crunch, crunch!

People in Colombia

top their hot dogs with

crushed potato chips.

From state to state, there are

many ways to eat a hot dog.

In Hawaii, fruits make

a sweet topping.

How do you like your hot dog?

Make Octopus Dogs

You won't find these under the sea. But octopus dogs make a fun meal. Be sure to ask an adult to help you cut and cook the hot dogs.

Makes 4 servings

Here's what you need:

Ingredients	*Tools*
4 hot dogs	knife
water (to boil hot dogs)	saucepan
ketchup, mustard	plates

Here's what you do:

1. Cut each hot dog almost in half length-wise, leaving about 2 inches (5 centimeters) uncut. This portion of the hot dog will serve as the octopus' head.
2. Carefully cut the hot dog half into eight strips. Now you have eight "legs." Repeat until all the hot dogs are cut.
3. Boil the hot dogs until cooked. The octopus legs will curl when boiled.
4. Place the cooked hot dogs on plates to look like octopuses. You can decorate the octopus dogs with ketchup and mustard.

Glossary

batter—a mixture consisting mainly of milk, eggs, flour, and cornmeal used to coat corn dogs

Coney Island—a vacation area of New York City; Coney Island has a beach and amusement park

corn dog—a hot dog dipped in cornmeal batter, fried, and served on a stick

grill—a grate on which food is broiled

soy—a substance made from soybeans

spice—a substance with a smell or taste used to flavor foods

Read More

Ipcizade, Catherine. *The Saucy Scoop on Pizza.* Favorite Food Facts. Mankato, Minn.: Capstone Press, 2012.

Sylver, Adrienne. *Hot Diggity Dog: The History of the Hot Dog.* New York: Dutton Childrens Books, 2010.

Internet Sites

FactHound offers a safe, fun way to find Internet sites related to this book. All of the sites on FactHound have been researched by our staff.

Here's all you do:

Visit *www.facthound.com*

Type in this code: 9781429666619

Super-cool stuff! Check out projects, games and lots more at www.capstonekids.com

Index

Word Count: 218
Grade: 1
Early-Intervention Level: 20